WOMEN OF DESTINY

25 CHALLENGES WOMEN FACE

ELEANOR CRAWFORD

Copyright © 2016 by Eleanor Crawford

All rights reserved. No part of this book may be reproduced or transmitted in any form or by any means without written permission of the author.

ISBN 978-0-935379-16-7

Library of Congress Control Number: 2016938955

Published by New Life Educational Services
P.O. Box 96
Oak Lawn, Illinois 60454

Printed in the U.S.A.

TABLE OF CONTENTS

Introduction 1
1. ABORTION 3
2. CHAUVINISM 5
3. CHURCH ABUSE 7
4. DEPRESSION 11
5. DIRECTION IN LIFE 13
6. DIVORCE 15
7. DOMESTIC VIOLENCE 16
8. DRUG ADDICTION 19
9. FRIENDSHIP BETRAYAL 21
10. HOMELESSNESS 25
11. INFERIORITY 27
12. INFERTILITY 30
13. LEADERSHIP 32
14. LONELINESS 34
15. MARRIAGE 36
16. PROMISCUITY 39
17. PRISON 41
18. RAPE 45
19. REBELLIOUS CHILDREN 47
20. REJECTION 50
21. SEXUAL HARASSMENT 52
22. SEX TRAFFICKING 55

23. SINGLE MOTHERS 57
24. STRESS 59
25. WAR 63
EPILOGUE 65
ABOUT THE AUTHOR 73

Introduction

Women around the world have seen a great deal of progress in the last 100 years. In the United States specifically, they have realized the right to vote, an equal rights amendment to the constitution, and the prohibition of sexual discrimination.

Despite all this progress inequality still exists. Women today are challenged by chauvinism and by the need to juggle all these new rights with a household that is still deemed as "women's work." They are victimized because of their inherent vulnerability, and they are taken advantage of in the workplace. Women still earn less while working just as hard as men.

Women are constantly challenged by violence, stereotypes, and poverty. More than 80% of reported violence are females. Millions of single mothers strive to provide for their children while fighting against poverty, but many of the cards are stacked against them. Girls are sexualized from a young age. Meanwhile women are simultaneously expected to advertise their availability, yet shunned and persecuted for using their female assets to get ahead. All these things culminate to reduce their potential to succeed. It also leaves behind traces of depression, a lack of confidence, and insecurity.

As you continue reading, you will learn more about the nature of these challenges. This book will also navigate some of the most difficult choices a woman must make over her lifetime. Education is one of the best weapons available. By learning what they are up against, women become empowered to overcome. Within you will learn strategies to rise above.

Establishing a politically correct and gender neutral society won't in itself solve the complexities of the economic and social challenges women face. The solution must come from deep beneath the surface. Women must define the expectations that hold them back, dispelling the negative gender stereotypes. In addition to that, women must also themselves join forces and work together, rather than tearing one another apart. Only then can they begin to break free.

Women also contend with many aspects of church abuse, which leaves them conflicted and devastated.

"There is neither Jew nor Greek, there is neither bond nor free, there is neither male or female, for ye are all in Christ Jesus." (Galatians 3:28)

"And I entreat thee also, true yokefellow, help those women which laboured with me in the gospel, with Clement also, and with other my fellow labourers, whose names are in the book of life." (Philippians 4:3)

1. ABORTION

Choosing whether to have an abortion is a difficult decision, no matter the reasoning behind it. A woman may be mentally or physically unable to care for a baby, or there might be medical factors that make abortion the only option. Regardless, every facet of abortion can be challenging. The barriers are many, and the after effects can be devastating, even when it seems like it is the best decision.

Barriers

In the United States, abortion is a legal medical procedure. The Congress of Obstetrics and Gynecologists assure us that abortion is sometimes vital to womens's health. However, that doesn't mean that an abortion is easy to procure. In just the last five years, over two hundred legal restrictions have been passed.

Mandatory waiting periods have been established as well as a restriction that the procedure must be completed before a woman reaches 20 gestational weeks. This means that a woman will need to consult with her doctor less than 13 weeks before the end of her last menstrual cycle. Additionally, there are strict guide lines regarding which doctors are permitted to perform them.

Abortions can also be financially costly. They aren't covered by insurance or Medicaid, though there are some specific exceptions. That leaves the out of pocket expense between three and nine hundred dollars, which pose a huge challenge for young or impoverished women.

After Effects and Complications

Women who receive abortions are left with a mountain of baggage to uncover. Physically, abortion can be a painful process, which often has dangerous complications. It can also reduce a woman's fertility and compromise future pregnancies. It shouldn't be a decision easily made.

Nonetheless, the related emotions often lead to depression, anxiety, and even suicidal tendencies. There can also be negative social implications, as it is controversial in some circles. It can be helpful to have Christian counseling before you make a decision to have an abortion.

"Thou shalt not kill." (Exodus 20:13)

"Lo, children are an heritage of the Lord and the fruit of the womb is his reward." (Psalm 127:3)

2. CHAUVINISM

While many advances have been made in the name of gender equality, chauvinism is still alive and well both at home and in the workplace. It flourishes in modes that many people aren't even aware of because it is so ingrained in society that we have grown blind, or apathetic, to its existence. Let's look at a few examples.

Employability

A recent study demonstrates why the glass ceiling is still firmly in place. Researchers set up an experiment that took a close look at how men and women analyzed job applicants for a hypothetical position. In the study, men showed a clear bias by consistently preferring male candidates, even when the female candidates had similar or better resumes. This means women may need to work twice as hard at creating a good impression to land their dream job.

Wage Gap

Even when women do manage to land the job, chauvinism still prevails. On average, males are paid two and a half times more than women. Some try to explain this away by saying that men pursue tougher jobs or are more ambitious, but that simply isn't true. An analysis showed that in a pool of nearly ten thousand nearly graduated MBA students,

The males received starting salaries that averaged $15,000 more than their female colleagues. This is seen in nearly every profession.

Housework

The feminist movement successfully created a pathway for women to leave the home and enter careers. Nonetheless, eighty percent of women report that they still complete more of the household chores than their spouses. For some reason, housework and childrearing are still predominately considered women's work.

For many women, this type of chauvinism is insurmountable. Fortunately, history shows that progress is possible. The first step is bringing greater amounts of attention to the inequalities. If you are disturbed by these examples, speak out against chauvinism. Don't let chauvinistic stigmas hold you back.

The daughters of Zelophehad challenged Moses, princes and elders of Israel against what they considered to be a great injustice. Moses took their cause to the Lord and God rendered a verdict in their favor. God said, "the daughters of Zelophehad speak right." (Numbers 27:1-9)

3. CHURCH ABUSE

Every year, millions of girls and women worldwide suffer violence. In some countries up to 70% of women have experienced physical and/or sexual violence in their lifetime from an intimate partner. Sadly this is happening in churches too.

Violence against women is a shocking reality that has pervaded most human cultures. Whether by turning a blind eye or subliminal religious pressure to turn the other cheek where Jesus would have confronted an evil. Violence against women has been too often unchallenged by the churches. Women aged 15-44 are more at risk from rape and domestic violence than from cancer, car accidents, war and malaria. Every year, millions of girls and women worldwide suffer violence and abuse from men in their lives whom they trust. Husbands, boyfriends; who are trusted with the intimate aspects of the lives of the women with whom they have a relationship. Men with whom women have romanced, dined and danced, believing their powerful words of love and affection. Men in whom trust has been deeply placed.

Sexual violence effects an estimated one and five women globally. The impact and consequences of an intimate violation of the body can result in extensive physical and psychological trauma, along with unwanted pregnancies. Sexual violence in conflict has been long recognized as a tactic of war. As no respecter of age, culture, ethnicity, or wealth, violence against women has its foundations in gender equality and discrimination against women. At its heart is the abuse of power and control over another individual.

In Churches Too

With one and three women globally suffering violence in her lifetime, this will mean women who have domestic abuse will be in churches too. Many through shame, stigma or the lack of a safe place to disclose that abuse, will remain and suffer in silence in our churches. God rarely overrides a person's will. A perpetrator of violence needs to recognize that they are choosing to abuse, that abuse is a choice, and acknowledge the damage it is causing to their victim as well as to themselves.

What can Churches do?

The first action churches can take, is to acknowledge the reality of the statistics and recognize that domestic abuse and violence against women happens in churches too. This can then lead into discussions and solutions offered by churches, depending on their own context and resources. Getting leaders and pastors to use theology and sermons to challenge abuse can make all the difference to a victim or a survivor, and can challenge perpetrators of abuse who may well be sitting in the congregation.

Giving a clear and authoritative message that all violence against women is wrong and must stop, breaks the myth that abuse cannot happen in the churches. Church leaders have a responsibility to teach theology well and clearly address mixed up or wrongly applied theology. This is particularly relevant, and possibly life saving, when addressing domestic abuse. Pastors need to be aware of a toxic combination of misinterpreted theology of submission, forgiveness and divorce that can leave a woman feeling powerless, unable to keep herself and the children safe, in a relationship where her husband is choosing to abuse her. Subconsiously or inadvertently the church can place the institution of marriage above life itself by saying a wife must stay with her husband thus placing her at risk of harm, and at worse death.

Education and Awareness

Church leaders, and particularly people involved in pastoral care, may find it useful to attend basic awareness training on domestic abuse, what it is and how to address it. Each church should have procedures safeguarding against domestic abuse, and a domestic violence referral line can be added, so that women who are abused know who they can contact in church and know that they will be listened to safely.

Policy and Procedure

The church operations manual can give information on its policies and procedures in regards to domestic abuse. This informs the congregation that the church is aware of the issue of domestic abuse and is prepared to take action. For victims and survivors coming into the church, it signals that the church is a safe place and for perpetrators that there is zero tolerance.

Link to Local Professional Services

It is important that churches, where possible and feasible, link into available local professional services. Supporting local safe houses within a set of agreed boundaries and guidelines, can be a real support to survivors of abuse who could be otherwise isolated and alone. Some churches have provided practical items for safe houses, noting that women have often left home with very little clothing or essentials.

Model Healthy Relationships

Congregations and church leaders can model positive healthy relationships that break cultural stereotypes and treat women with dignity and respect, as made in the image of God.

They can commit not to shy away from a standing against a culture that diminishes and denigrates women, and to challenge others when women are treated as less than made in God's image.

Violence against women is pervasive in all cultures, and churches are not excluded from the problem. It is vital that churches rise to the challenge and take their place in responding well to survivors, offering space and also providing accountability and support to perpetrators of abuse as they take responsibility for their attitudes and actions. Churches should not do this alone, but actively seek out the advice and professional services where they are available and accessible. It is important that bridges are built with professional services, to improve mutual understanding and establish a referral process for situations of abuse when these arise. May the church rise up to take action! Christians must rise up and make a stand and say, "This is our business, this is our church." All violence against women is wrong and must stop!

4. DEPRESSION

Depression is on the rise nationwide. Females are seventy percent more likely to be affected. Hormonal differences are partly to blame. Ladies experience highs and lows thanks to hormonal shifts during pregnancy or menopause. These chemical imbalances add to the stress of trying to juggle careers and domestic duties. Once a woman recognizes that she is suffering from depression, there are many unfortunate challenges that may prevent her from getting the treatment she needs.

Ineffective Treatments

Research from Wayne State University found that less than fifty percent of all U.S. citizens diagnosed with depression actually get treated. Even then, only about one in five receives treatment that aligns with modern standards. It is not surprising then that more than half don't respond to the first type of treatment they receive.

There are many factors that act as barriers, keeping women from the right treatment. Two are discussed here:

Lack of Health Insurance

Access to health care often corresponds to a patient's socioeconomic condition. Studies show a clear connection between poverty and poor physical and mental health. In a struggling economy, many cannot afford health insurance. The majority of those individuals are women. Statistics show that households run by single women are less likely to have access to sufficient mental health services.

Shame and Embarassment

Depression is a disease that doesn't discriminate. Still, research suggests that women, especially black women, experience depression differently than other segments of the population. This is partially because women have trouble admitting they need help. It is also influenced by the taboo spotlight in which mental health is seen, particularly in the African-American community. These women are less likely to seek treatment because they feel ashamed or embarrassed.

The Bright Side

In spite of these hurdles, women have expressed an impressive ability to develop alternative coping mechanisms, often involving family, community, or religion.

And the mental health community is hopeful that, through expanded awareness, the attitudes surrounding depression will change, encouraging more women to seek treatment sooner.

5. DIRECTION IN LIFE

Life is complex. Between working hard, saving money, buying houses, and raising children, there is also a lot of stress. It is not uncommon that, in the midst of all that stress, women start to wonder whether they are moving in the right direction. What are you really working towards? Many women find themselves standing still, waiting for the right answer to appear. Here you will find four simple strategies that will assist you in finding direction in life.

Stop Analyzing

The fastest way to alleviate some of that stress and frustration is to stop overthinking. When you focus too much on analyzing how you should be spending your life, you end up wasting a lot of time and creating unnecessary stress. Women tend to over analyze, which can be valuable at times, but can lead to sleepless nights, burn out, and more questions than answers. When you focus more attention on the present, you will open up far more possibilities.

Get Active

Odds are, when you were spending so much time analyzing, you were also standing still. As you start taking action, you will instantly feel empowered. Move, ask questions, explore your choices, and work towards something. Working is more rewarding than thinking because you can see the progress unfold. You cannot control tomorrow, but you can control how you spend your time right now. When you get active, every step will move you closer to the direction you need to travel.

Be Intuitive

Sometimes, feeling is better than knowing. You don't actually need all the facts in order to know intuitively whether a certain path brings you happiness or discomfort, instead of burying yourself in information, allow your intuition to guide the way.

Trust Yourself

You won't always be able to rely on the reactions of friends or loved ones to judge the merit of a direction you choose. Instead, you must trust yourself. Trust your intuition and your own judgment.

Trust your path. If it feels right, then it probably is. Trust yourself to find the strength to overcome all of the challenges along the way.

Trust God

"Trust in the Lord with all thine heart; and lean not to thine own understanding, in all thy ways acknowledge Him and He shall direct thy paths," (Proverbs 3:5-6)

"The steps of a good man are ordered by the Lord and He delighted in His way." (Psalm 37:23)

6. DIVORCE

Almost all divorced women experience a difficult time shortly after the relationship is over. It will be crucial for you to understand the potential effects of divorce or separation and develop a practical perception of what will happen in the upcoming days.

Monetary Hardships

It is common to experience financial problems following a divorce, especially if a woman has previously been a stay at home mom. Establishing financial independence while caring for a family is not always a seamless transition, but it can be done.

When considering divorce, be sure to do some careful financial planning. Line up a job, create a realistic budget, and stick to it.

Emotional Struggles

It is inevitable that divorce will leave a woman with overwhelming emotions such as anger, hurt, bitterness, resentment, disappointment, or loneliness. This can be the case even if the divorce was her idea. Expect that you will need some time to rest and recover emotionally.

The only way to get through this struggle is to recognize and accept the emotions in a healthy way, a therapist might be able to help. Eventually, allow yourself to release the negative feelings or resentments so that you are able to move forward in a healthy way.

7. DOMESTIC VIOLENCE

Those who hardly understand the dynamics of domestic violence believe that a victim can just leave her abuser whenever she wants to. "Why don't you just leave, if its that bad?" Leaving an abusive relationship is very hard to do. A woman facing domestic violence does not stay in the relationship because she likes the abuse. There are numerous reasons as to why a woman stays with her abuser. Fear, no money, no support system, the children, immigration issues, addiction, disability, having no self-esteem/self-confidence, etc.. The abuse does not always end once she has left the relationship.

Challenges

Fear

- Fear for her own life and the lives of those she loves. (The abuser has threatened to commit suicide or to kill her, children, family, friends, or pets if she leaves.)

- Fear that no one believes her (The abuser appears as a good person in public.)

- Fear that the abuser will take the children away or call social services.

- Fear that the abuser will find her (That's what happened the other times she left. Why would this time be different?)

- Fear that he would always be looking over her shoulder wherever she goes because no one can guarantee her safety if she leaves.

- She may also fear she will never have another relationship if this one ends.

- Fear that the abuser will deny the abuse when asked about it and that others will blame the victim or think she is crazy,

- Fear of losing societal or socioeconomic staus.

Finance

- The victim may have a little or no work skills and wonders how to find employment that will enable her/him to provide adequate shelter, food, clothing, and child care for her/his family.

- The victim may have been fired from previous employment due to the abuser's ongoing harassment on the job or absentism due to injuries or emotional stress suffered in the relationship. Therefore, it could be difficult to find new employment.

- The victim may have little or no access to cash. The abuser makes all the financial decisions and controls all the money and important financial documents.

- The victim may believe that as long as the children have a roof over their heads, food on the table, and clothes on their backs, she/he can stand the abuse.

- The victim is depressed, making it difficult to take action.

- The victim believes in rigid female/male roles in relationships where the male is "king of his castle" and has the right to do whatever he wants in his own home.

- The victim may lack resources to leave abusive partners and start new lives. This includes affordable and dignified housing, child care, health care, and adequate paid employment.

8. DRUG ADDICTION

Women suffer from the devastating physical and emotional consequences of addiction to alcohol or drugs, but many studies have shown that women in particular face several hurdles and barriers in identifying addiction, seeking treatment, and receiving effective treatment to help them overcome the addiction. Here are some of the unique challenges that women face. Women face tougher challenges. They tend to progress more quickly from using an addictive substance to dependence

(a phenomenon known as telescoping). They also develop medical or social consequences of addiction faster than men, often find it harder to quit using addictive substances, and are more susceptible to relapse. These gender differences can affect treatment.

Nicotine

Nearly 71 million Americans ages 12 and older 23% of women—said they smoked tobacco (most often cigarettes).

Female smokers face more health risks than male smokers; they may be more likely to develop lung cancer, for example, and are twice as likely to have a heart attack. But the research suggests that women find it more difficult than men to quit smoking, and more likely to start smoking again even if they quit.

The reasons for this are not clear. Although studies have found that female smokers are more responsive to environmental cues and triggers (such as wanting to light up a cigarette when drinking alcohol), while male smokers are more responsive to the biological effects of nicotine. This suggests –preliminary research confirms—that nicotine replacement therapy may not work as well in women as it does in men. A meta-analysis of 14 placebo-controlled studies concluded that although both women and men were more likely to quit smoking while using a nicotine patch, women were less likely than men to do so. About 20% of men quit for 6 months using the patch, compared with nearly 15% of women; with a placebo patch, roughly 10% of both sexes quit.

Finally, studies find that kicking the habit is especially tough for women during the menstrual cycle's luteal phase (which begins mid-cycle, just after ovulation). Preliminary research suggests that women who time their quit date to occur during the follicular phase (which begins after menstruation and ends at ovulation) are more likely to abstain from cigarettes for a longer period than women who quit during the luteal phase.

9. FRIENDSHIP BETRAYAL

Friendship betrayal is one of the most painful human experiences. Discovering that someone we trusted has deeply hurt us pulls the reality rug from us. When we see the word "betrayal" we may immediately think " affair." But betrayal comes in many forms. Abandonment, vicious gossip, and spreading lies also may be experienced as betrayal.

A damaging aspect of betrayal is that our sense of reality is undermined. What felt like solid trust suddenly crumbles. Our innocence is shattered. We're left wondering: What happened? How could this happen? Who is this person? Some betrayals leave us with little choice but to heal and move on with our lives, such as when we're suddenly abandoned.

Context of Betrayal

Friendship betrayal, is one major challenge women face. It may occur in any kind of relationship context if one or other parties violates salient relational expectations or "break the rules" in some ways.

Close friends, for example, hold mutual expectations about one another's behavior's based on shared understandings of the rules of friendship. Such rules typically include respecting privacy, volunteering help when needed, not criticizing one another in public and sharing confidences but not disclosing them to others. Violating any of the friendship rules may be appraised as a betrayal and lead to the break down of the relationship. Most times, women get to be betrayed by their girl friends almost as frequently as by spouses.

Way Forward

Betrayal is not a nice thing to have to deal with and at its worse it can be devastating. It can throw our lives into a tail spin and shatter our assumptions. However, there are things we can do that will help us deal with betrayal and move forward with our lives.

Realize You Are Not Alone

Betrayal can be very hard to come terms with, but it is not uncommon. It can happen to anyone and it's been going on since time immemorial, no one is immune, even Jesus was eventually betrayed. Betrayal is an unfortunate characteristic of human nature and even your closest friends can be quick to betray you if aroused by envy. Sometimes we can be betrayed by those who we think should be showing us gratitude for all the help we have provided them in the past.

Friendship betrayal is not always obvious either, sometimes the signs are there but we give people the benefit of the doubt or we are in denial. At other times there are no signs and this type of behavior can be all the more difficult to deal with.

Accept How You Feel

Apart from being initially shell-shocked by what has happened, you will have to come to terms and find a way to mitigate the damage already done. Sometimes we can find ourselves going back to the very core of a hurtful situation, perhaps we are in denial about what really occurred, or we wish things could go back to how they were before the betrayal. I have been in a situation where I was betrayed by a group of people who not only stabbed me in the back, but conspired against me and yet I wanted to go back into the very heart of it. I wanted to be accepted again. I thought I could rebuild the trust. I soon realized that I could not get what I thought I needed from this group of people, and never would. The damage had been done and things would never be the same again. Accepting these emotions and feeling my pain was part of the healing process. At this stage it is helpful to talk through your feelings with a friend, a professional counselor, or even the perpetrator themselves if the situation calls for it.

Don't Retalliate

Feelings at such times can be very intense as we are confused, hurt and bewildered, our emotions are still raw and so they can make us irrational. Give yourself time and space to assess the situation and try your hardest to be objective. Dealing with betrayal and coming to terms with the hurt inflicted on you by people who you love and trust is a huge thing. So first and foremost be kind to yourself. Although it is normal to want to retaliate and seek revenge for the hurt you have suffered, this will not be to anyone's benefit. Don't stoop to their level, instead act with integrity.

Learn From It

Betrayal teaches you not only about other people but also about yourself. Did you allow others to constantly cross boundaries, or borrow money from you? Did you call them to account when they crossed the line? The more people push and the more you give in, the messier it usually is in the end.

Learn From It

Accept what is and learn from it. However, it is important that you refrain from blaming yourself for betrayal; it usually has little to do with you and everything to do with the perpetrator.

If you are going to carry on with the relationship, you do need to understand why the betrayal happened in the first place to prevent it from happening again. It might be that the person suffered from low self esteem, it could be just a mistake, it could be anything. The important thing is that you don't take it personally and free yourself from blame. Otherwise you will carry this distrust with you into other relationships. Learn accept and move on.

Forgive

Forgiveness does not mean you are a walkover and that you condone what happened to you. It doesn't mean that everything in the garden is rosy and that you have to transcend into some kind of ethereal plane of enlightenment. It doesn't even mean you have to reconcile with the person that betrayed you. What it does mean is that we change our perception of how we view the situation, instead of viewing it from anger and holding onto hot coals, we accept what has happened and come from a place of understanding . Forgiveness is for you to drop all your emotional baggage. Try to understand that not everyone who betrays you has done so intentionally or comes from a place of malice, it may be that there were other reasons, they just couldn't help themselves or did it out of fear. Forgiveness is about your own inner healing.

"Yea, mine own familiar friend, in whom I trusted, which did eat of my bread, hath lifted up his heel against me." (Psalm 41:9)

"Then came Peter to him, and said Lord, how oft shall my brother sin against me, and I forgive him? Till seven times. Jesus saith unto him, I say not unto thee, Until seven times: but, Until seventy times seven." (Matthew 18:21-22)

10. HOMELESSNESS

Homeless women are susceptible to the same problems faced by people who do have homes, their habitats make dealing with these issues far more challenging. Still some conditions are more common in homeless women. For example, a recent study showed that 80% of homeless women experience a chronic medical problem.

Here are some of their biggest challenges including violence, exposure, hygiene, mental illnesses, reproductive health, and malnutrition.

Exposure

Homeless women are more vulnerable to the elements. When temperatures dip, they often develop frostbite or hypothermia. There have even been reports of homeless women freezing to death. Warm weather can be just as dangerous, leading to dehydration, sunburn, or heatstroke. There is also an increased risk of getting hit by a vehicle.

Violence

Women who are homeless witness and experience more violence. At least forty percent of all homeless people have been assaulted at least once. Still worse, an estimated 25% of all homeless women have been victims of rape.

Malnutrition

These women lack the financial means to acquire sufficient quantities of healthy foods. Food banks and homeless shelters try to help, but it isn't enough. Poor nutrition can lead to malnutrition, dizziness, weakness, fatigue and chronic health problems.

Sexual and Reproductive Health

Studies suggest that homeless women are at a greater risk for developing sexually transmitted infections and diseases. Their habitat and finances make it difficult to seek medical care, making pregnancy far more dangerous and stressful.

Mental Health

Approximately 75% of all homeless women are challenged by mental health problems. Most suffer from depression, and more than 60% have contemplated suicide. Most of these women lack the

Strong support systems that are essential to mental health and escaping homelessness.

11. INFERIORITY

It's hard to fathom why, after two thousand years of civilization, women are still considered inferior to men by most cultures, whether in developed, developing, or undeveloped nations.

Why is the thought of electing a woman president of the United States so unthinkable to most of the population? Why is it surprising that most Fortune 1000 companies still lack a woman on their board of directors? Why do women athletes still lack funding and popular support on a scale that their male counter parts garner?

Because after 2,000 years of recorded history, and 20,000 years of artifact-preserved history, women have generally been relegated as breeders not leaders.

And even though technological and economical advances have allowed women to have children as well as professional careers, their multimillenial image as background breeders persists.

Throughout the church's history, women have been considered inferior by nature and by law. Greek philosophy which was adopted by christians, held women to be inferior to men by nature. Roman law which became the basis for the church's laws, gave women a low status in society. Women did not enjoy equal rights in their homes and in civic society. Some fathers of the church linked women's presumed inferior status to scriptural texts: only the man they said was created in God's image. Moreover Paul had forbidden women to teach in church. "Church orders" of the first millennium also show traces of the belief in women's inferiority. Knowing this background, we need not be surprised to find that the vast majority of fathers, canon lawyers, theologians and church leaders were of the opinion that such an inferior person could not be ordained a priest. It is clear that this social and cultural bias invalidated their judgment as to the suitability of women for ordination.

According to Plato (427-347 B.C), women came about through a physical degeneration of the human being." It is only males who are created directly by the Gods and are given souls. Those who are rightly return to the stars, but those who are 'cowards' [lead unrighteous lives] may with reason be supposed to have changed into the nature of women in the second generation."

Similarly, Aristotle (384-322) considered women 'defective human beings. "The reason why the man dominates in society is his superior intelligence. Only the man is a full human being. The relationship between the male and female is by nature such that the male is higher. The female lower, that the male rules and the female is ruled."

In Roman civil law too, women's rights were very limited. The reasons given in Roman law for restraining women's rights are variously described as the weakness of her sex or the stupidity of her sex. The context makes clear that the problem did not lie in women's physical weakness, but in what was perceived as her lack of sound judgment and her inability to think logically.

Less widely known is that many evolutionists, including Darwin, taught that women were biologically and intellectually inferior to men. The intelligence gap that Darwinists believed existed between males and females were not minor, but of a level that caused some evolutionists to classify the sexes as two distinct psychological species, males as homo frontalis and females as homo parietalis. Darwin himself concluded that the differences between male and female humans were so enormous that he was amazed that such different beings belong to the same species and he was surprised that even greater differences still had not been evolved.

This pervasive fallacy continues to limit the creative potential of half of the world's population. The underlying belief in women's inferiority seems to be so ingrained in our collective psyches that even the media doesn't seem motivated to investigate—let alone challenge—its roots.

"Beware lest any man spoil you through philosophy and vain deceit, after the tradition of men, after the rudiments of the world, and not after Christ." (Colossians 2:8)

12. INFERTILITY

There are few things that threaten a woman's sense of purpose more than infertility. Many women dream of becoming mothers from an early age. When that doesn't end up being easy, or even possible, it can be crushing. This becomes a huge challenge to accept and overcome through multiple facets, many of them deeply emotional.

Equilibrium

It can be difficult to balance your emotions enough to continue with daily life when you are rolling through the coaster of infertility. There are numerous treatments, which present both hope and the possibility of devastating disappointment. Still, it is important to find a balance between staying realistic and seeking a miracle.

Pride

Childbearing is supposed to be a natural thing that women do. It can be difficult admitting something is wrong and seeking help. The nature of fertility can create embarrassing circumstances that a woman must weather through, often pushing ego aside.

Forgiveness

Accepting infertility is important to moving forward. You can't start to embracing solutions or alternatives if you are still full of anger towards yourself, your body, or your genetics. Many things in life aren't fair. Women with infertility must rediscover how to love themselves and forgive their bodies.

Letting Go

The biggest challenge of fertility is realizing that it is out of your control. You may not have control over how your body responds to the fertility treatments you choose, even if you carefully follow all your doctor's advice. Do what you can and seek out other options. A big part of moving past infertility is acknowledging it and looking for a miracle. There are numerous ways of becoming a mother.

"...all things are possible to him that believeth."

(Mark 9:23)

13. LEADERSHIP

Women who seek leadership must blast through the preexisting gaps. Two of the biggest gaps are represented by inequalities in access to promotions and power. They are further exacerbated by chauvinism and hypocritical messages, adding complexity to the simplistic vision of feminine progress.

The Threat of Ambition

Research shows that assertive women in leadership are more likely to be seen as aggressive rather than ambitious. Women often fail to ask for exactly what they want. But when they do, they are seen as pushy or domineering, leaving their male counterparts feeling threatened rather than helpful. If women are to rise in the ranks, there needs to be a change of perception.

Networks

While females excel at social networking, studies suggest that they struggle to utilize these networks effectively. They shy from exploring relationships to promote themselves because it feels wrong. This creates a disadvantage when they compete against men, who are more likely to ask for sponsors or jobs in exchange for social currency.

Financial Chauvinism

One way to assume a leadership role is to start your own company. Women are excellent business leaders, but they don't always get an opportunity to shine. Studies show that women are less likely to gain financial backing for a startup company. This persists despite the fact that more successful startups have women in senior positions. Women do well when they are given a chance.

Staying True

Women in leadership positions often struggle to maintain their own style of leading, instead mimicking the way they see men lead. Ironically, in doing this they discard their greatest assets, their ability to collaborate, listen, and foster positive working relationships. These are all skills needed by the greatest role models. Women would do well to embrace their natural leadership qualities, allowing them more authority and persuasiveness.

14. LONELINESS

Loneliness is bigger in size than depression. Why? Because depression creeps in only when a person feels lonely! And therefore it won't be wrong to say that depression is a side effect of loneliness, whereas loneliness, is one long fledged problem.

The question is, with people reaching from one part of the world to another in mere hours and being able to contact each other, no matter how far apart they live, in fractions of seconds. Why have people started to feel lonelier than before? Why have people, with the world shrinking more and more everyday—are feeling lost and depressed.

Women fall into these dungeons more easily than men, because for some reason they make their relationships the center of their lives. Men on the other hand, treat every relationship with equal emotions and maturity and therefore do not fall as deep when they find themselves with a heart breaking situation.

But women, as soon as they fall in love, distance themselves from every possible relationship and pines down their love, hopes and ideas to one man entirely. That is why when the man leaves her she has no one to go to.

Loneliness can be treated by developing your social skills. Yes, if you are lonely, why not go out and join a dance class, singing class, writing class, or to church. This will help you improve yourself.

Loneliness can be treated by keeping yourself busy with useful work. You can always sit down and read a good book. Reading expands your mind and teaches you how to fight serious problems like loneliness and depression. For a woman it is very important that she keeps company with only good people because good company will help you maintain your bearings.

"Casting all of your care upon him; for he careth for you."

(1 Peter 5:7)

15. MARRIAGE

Women look forward to their wedding day, expecting it to be the best and most beautiful day of their lives. The plans take months, if not years. Unfortunately, all that planning cannot guarantee a perfect marriage. In fact, even the best marriage can be challenging, exhausting, and disheartening at times. Here you will find five of the most common marriage challenges women face.

In-Laws

Relationships with in-laws can be uncomfortably complex, especially if they are the meddling type.

The result can mean countless arguments with your spouse. Despite hard feelings, it is important to establish a positive rapport with in-laws for the benefit of your spouse, your offspring, and your own peace. Being aware of potential conflicts can help you react more respectfully and rationally.

Money

Another reason married couples tend to argue is over money. You can avoid a lot of tension by making each other's expectations clear from the beginning and maintaining open communication.

It is a good idea to establish goals and limits. Agree to discuss purchases over a certain price point. Spending effects both of your futures, be sure neither party is left out of the discussion, regardless of who earns more.

Traditions

Combining holiday traditions can be difficult, particularly if you and your spouse come from divergent cultures or religions. Sit down and allow each other to voice which traditions are most important to you, but be willing to compromise to create a tradition the whole family can enjoy without tension.

Raising Children

While having children is a blessing, they do come with a great deal of physical and emotional stress. A woman should expect sleepless nights, hormonal changes, and discipline challenges. A couple might also disagree about how the children are to be raised and the expectations placed upon them. It is ideal that these types of discussions are explored before marriage to ensure that your ideas can work together.

While being married can present numerous challenges, you will also find it appealing and satisfying. Marriage can bring some of the most rewarding experiences. If you wish to create a lasting and fulfilling marriage, you will need to be willing to weather the storms along the way. Communication is the key.

Moving Forward

You will eventually reach a point when you are ready to let go of the past and build a new life. Navigating this transition can be slippery. Allow yourself to become open to the possibility of a future that is bright and different. When you start to consider new relationships, try to leave past hurts or trust issues behind.

The key to healing and moving forward after a divorce is believing that life can get better. Believe in yourself and the power of God. Doing this will help you push through every challenge you face. Be patient and kind with yourself as well as with others.

16. PROMISCUITY

One of the biggest challenges that women face in modern society can be traced to the promiscuity double standard. The problem is that females are simultaneously encouraged to exploit their physical attributes and yet are penalized for doing so. We have created a climate in which women are pressured to dress and act seductively in order to get what they want (attention, money, relationships, fame, etc.), and then they are judged or obstracized for their promiscuity.

Value

Women are constantly reminded that their value is measured according to their sexuality and availability. It isn't uncommon for them to receive harassment in the form of catcalls as they walk down the street. When they complain of such treatment they are told to look upon the unwanted banner as a compliment. How has society come to twist sexual harassment into a compliment?

Our culture subconsciously emphasizes male desires. Women who don't play into these desires are labeled ugly, cold, or prudish. Other women have learned to exploit those desires for personal gain.

Although this can be successful in the short term, in the long run it can further devalue females, perpetuating a broken system.

Shame

It is ironic that a culture that places such an emphasis on feminine sexuality and availability does not embrace the women who represent such ideals. In fact, women who portray promiscuity are met with shame for expressing or acting upon those impulses. They are demeaned and labeled as sluts while their male counterparts are praised. Suitors often judge women as not being suitable for marriage if they "put out" too soon, yet those same men never label themselves as unsuitable husbands.

A Better Way

Women must manage a difficult balance in a world where they are measured in sexual currency. In essence, women can't seem to win regardless of whether they shun or embrace the expectations placed upon them. Perhaps a better solution is to challenge the way we define value. We should give our expectations to God and realize an abundant life.

17. PRISON

Women in prison face many problems, some resulting from their lives prior to imprisonment, others resulting from their imprisonment itself. Women in prison have experienced victimization, unstable family life, school and work failure, and substance abuse and mental health problems.

Social factors that marginalize their participation in mainstream society and contribute to the rising number of women in prison include poverty, minority group member, single motherhood, and homelessness. While in U.S. prisons, women like prisoners throughout the world, face specific pains and deprivations arising directly from their imprisonment. Criminologists have argued that the prison system is ill-equipped to deal with these problems and that these issues are better managed outside the punitive environment of the prison. Without attention to these issues, women are then released from prison unprepared to manage their preexisting problems as well as those created by their imprisonment. There are several critical problems faced by women in prison, most are unmet in the prison environment.

Major Challenges

Separation from children and significant others. National surveys of women prisoners find that three-fourths of them were mothers, with two-thirds having children under the age of eighteen, Bloom and Chesney-Lind argue that mothers in prison face multiple problems in maintaining relationships with their children and encounter obstacles created both by the correctional system and child welfare agencies. The distance between the prison and the children's homes, lack of transportation, and limited economic resources compromise a woman prisoner's ability to maintain these relationships. Children of women in prison experience many hardships. Children may be traumatized by the arrest of their mother and the sudden forced separation imprisonment brings. Emotional reactions such as anger, anxiety, depression, and aggression have been found in the children of incarcerated mothers. While most children of incarcerated mothers live with relatives—typically grandparents—a small percentage of these children are placed in the child welfare system. These conditions compound the problem of maintaining contact with children. Over half of the women responding to Bloom and Steinhart's 1993 survey of imprisoned mothers reported never receiving visits from their children.

An estimated 4 to 9 percent of women come to prison pregnant. Women who give birth while incarcerated are rarely allowed to spend time with their child after birth. Mother infant bonding is severely undermined by this lack of contact after birth. Bedford Hills, a women's prison in New York, is the only program in the U.S. that allows women to keep their newborns with them in a special prison program. This humane response is more common in Britain and other European nations.

Most correctional systems do not take into account the importance of the mother-child relationship in designing policy for women in prison. Some states, such as New York and California, have begun innovative programs to address these problems. Coordinating visits to the prison and support services with child welfare agencies, providing special visiting areas, developing effective parenting classes, and developing community corrections programs for mothers and their children are examples of these innovations. Termination of parental rights also affect prison mothers. About half the states have policies that address the termination of parental rights of incarcerated parents. Advocates of women in prison and their children argue that family reunification, rather than termination of the mother's parental rights, should be a priority of correctional policy for women prisoners.

Lack of Substance Abuse Treatment

Although women offenders are very likely to have an extensive history of drug and alcohol use, a relatively small percentage of women receive any treatment within the justice system. Insufficient individual assessment, limited treatment for pregnant, mentally ill, and violent women offenders, and a lack of appropriate treatment and vocational training limit the effectiveness of the few programs that exist.

Physical and Mental Health Care

In addition to requiring basic health care, women offenders often have specific health needs related to their risky sexual and drug using behavior prior to imprisonment. Acoca has argued that the enormity of health care issues may in fact eclipse other correctional concerns as the female inmate population continues to grow. Women in prison are also at risk for infectious disease, including HIV, tuberculosis, sexually transmitted diseases, and hepatitis B and C infections. Problems of pregnant inmates include lack of prenatal and postnatal care, inadequate education regarding childbirth and parenting, and little or no preparation for the mother's separation from the infant after delivery.

Mental health disorders are equally neglected in U.S. prisons. While the prevalence and incidence of these needs are still to be determined, estimates suggest that 25 percent to 60 percent of the female prison population require mental health services.

Vocation and Educational Programs

In addition to insufficient substance abuse and mental health services, educational and vocational programs are also in short supply. Several studies (Pollock-Byrne; Morash, Haarr, and Rucker) found that female prisons offered fewer vocational and educational program opportunities when compared to those offered in male institutions. In general, women across the country lack training needed to obtain jobs that pay a living wage.

Sexual Abuse

The patterns of sexual abuse and coercion established in the early days of women's imprisonment continue in the contemporary era. Human Rights Watch examined this serious problem in their review of sexual abuse in selected U.S. prisons. The damage of the abuse itself is compounded by four specific issues: (1) the inability to escape one's abuser; (2) ineffectual or nonexistent investigative and grievance procedures; (3) lack of employee accountability (either criminally or administratively); and (4) little or no public concern. The report bluntly states that the findings indicate that being a woman in a U.S. state prison can be a terrifying experience.

18. RAPE

Rape can destroy a woman's physical and mental health, and even their desire to live. Society faces a huge challenge in working to reduce its occurrence and care for its victims. The first step is bringing the epidemic out into the open.

In the United States, studies show that approximately 270,000 females are sexually assaulted every year. It is not just inside this country. Rape culture exists around the globe. Rape is clearly a problem, and the consequences can linger for a lifetime.

Mental Health Challenges

One in three rape victims demonstrates symptoms of PTSD (post traumatic stress disorder). While some get better with time and therapy, one in ten are unable to escape it entirely. PTSD makes every day a challenge.

Thirty percent of female rape victims report feelings of serious depression. Comparing this to the occurrence of depression in the general population, which is approximately ten percent, shows that rape victims are at three times the normal risk for major depression.

The psychological effects can run deeper than anxiety or sadness. Rape victims are thirteen times more likely to report suicidal thoughts after the assault. Unfortunately, for some women, thoughts turn into actions.

Substance Abuse

It is not uncommon for women to turn to chemical substances to numb the trauma after a sexual assault. Rape victims are more likely to abuse drugs and alcohol. Compared to non-victims, these women are twenty six times more likely to develop dependency.

Resisting the Blame or Stigma

Nearly seventy percent of all rape victims worry that they will be blamed more than their attacker. Unfortunately, these fears are well-founded as society seeks to rationalize the crimes away. Many women find themselves ostracized by friends and even relatives.

Sexually Ttransmitted Diseases

Rape victims are often left with physical health problems. In addition to immediate traumas, they may also contract sexually transmitted diseases, sometimes including HIV or AIDS. Additionally, many women fear they will become pregnant as a result. Some do end up having to weight the options between abortion or raising a child that shares DNA with their attacker.

19. REBELLIOUS CHILDREN

Teen rebellion usually triggers some kind of emotional response. It can ignite fear in the hearts of parents who have children on the brink of adolescence; it can prompt both defensiveness and despair in the hearts of parents struggling through the teen years; and it can inspire a sigh of relief for parents who now have adult children. Whether your teen is opposing your authority or God's, rebellion is never easy to deal with.

Causes of Rebellion

- Parental discord
- Parental discipline methods
- Peer influence
- Fear of failure
- Low self worth
- Bitterness
- Desire to be independent

Characteristics of Rebellion

Rebellion takes place in the context of closed communication channels. There is a lack of constructive discussion, and the relationship becomes increasingly strained over time.

Rebellion features sudden, extreme expressions of independence. Defiant outbursts are common, and explosive anger surfaces.

Rebellion leads to a lack of mutual trust. The teen may be flagrantly dishonest and deceptive. They are caught in lies as they attempt to cover up or explain away their actions.

Rebellion results in increasing restrictions, explanations and discipline. Instead of discovering the necessity and wisdom the family standards that have been set up, the youth becomes more persistent in pushing against the limits.

Rebellion is marked by bitterness. Barriers of anger and withdrawal continue to build up between the teen and the parents, and the rebellion snowballs.

Coping with rebellion: Every teen's quest for freedom and lack of responsibility.

Once we have understood the nature of our teen's rebellion, we are ready to begin dealing with it. Approaches will vary based on the seriousness and type of behavior that is occurring, but here are some basic principles to keep in mind.

Practice loving and consistent discipline early. Inconsistent discipline encourages kids to test the limits, to see what they can get away with; Instead discipline in a way that your kids can know exactly what the rules are and what to expect when they break them—and above all, assure them of your unending love and support even when you are disappointed by their behavior.

Continue to set limits, but gradually work toward reasonable responsibility and decision making opportunities. Decide in advance which hills you are ready to stand on, and which areas have more room for flexibility. Remember that your ultimate goal is to release your child to live their own life.

Work on being approachable, flexible and understanding. Allow exceptions when you can, be willing to change, and apologize for your mistakes.

Create a safe environment for your teen to take risks to grow, and be a safe landing place when they fall.

Seek to provide adequate substitutes for banned activities or practices; don't continue to prohibit without providing an alternative.

Take time for and spend time with your teen! Do fun things together, attend their activities and show your interest. They don't need less of you during the teen years, but more.

20. REJECTION

Nobody takes rejection well; especially not women! Rejection in a wider context or in the context, of a man, is heart wrenching for women.

Why do I say that men, in most of the cases, take rejection better than women?

It is because women are more emotional and they think more from their hearts than their minds; they are more and more driven by their hormones and emotions and aren't at times able to tell between warm and cold.

Rejection comes from many sources in life:

- Men
- Women
- Children
- Teenagers
- Family
- Friends
- Work environment
- Social interactions and transactions

Rejection is overwhelming and devastating and its ultimate impact can produce suicide.

Rejection is part of life, it is inevitable. Keep in mind that even successful women have been in their lifetimes rejected by someone; but that did not stop them from rising and following their dreams. Therefore, my suggestion to you would be to work hard, live life like a queen who helps people stand up and not like a princess in distress.

21. SEXUAL HARASSMENT

Sexual harassment is one of the major problems facing our schools, businesses and corporations of the world. The definition of sexual harassment is any unwanted or inappropriate sexual attention. This includes touching, comments, or gestures. A key part of sexual harassment is that it is one sided and unwanted. There is a great difference between sexual harassment and romance or friendship, since those are mutual feelings of two people. Often sexual harassment makes the victim feel guilty, but it is important for the victim to remember that it is not their fault, the fault lies totally on the person who is the harasser.

Many times fear is involved in sexual harassment because it isn't about physical attraction, its about power. In fact, many sexual harassment incidents take place when one person is in a position of power over the other, or when a woman has an untraditional job such as a police officer, factory worker, business executive, or any other traditionally male job. Typical victims of sexual harassment are young, single, college-educated, members of a minority racial or ethnic group, in a trainee position, or have an immediate supervisor of the opposite sex. Sexual harassment is one-sided and unwelcome. Here are some of the most common challenges faced by sexually harassed women.

Reluctant to Complain

Sometimes sexually harassed women feel uncomfortable with what is happening to them but are reluctant to complain about it. There are many reasons for this, such as:

- They may be afraid of losing their job or facing other negative consequences.

- They do not want to be perceived as not having a sense of humor.

- They are afraid of the effect it would have on their long term career prospects.

- They are afraid of the effect that a formal complaint and investigation will have on themselves and their families.

- They do not want anyone to get in trouble.

- They think they are the ones with the problem.

- They believe they would be told that they are overreacting.

- They think that if they ignore the behavior it will go away.

- They are too embarrassed to talk about it.

- They don't want to be accused of not being a team player.

- They may feel they have to accept it, because that's the way things are.

- They don't want to be rejected or singled out by their co-workers.

- Another employee complained and nothing was done or the employee suffered negative consequences.

- They don't want to be labeled as troublemakers.

The sexually harassed woman's biggest fears is that the complaint won't be kept confidential. Sexual harassment often involves some very embarrassing events and victims generally do not want others to know what has happened to them.

Sexual harassment is always wrong. No one deserves it.

22. SEX TRAFFICKING

Sex trafficking is a contemporary form of slavery. It depicts the coercion of women through sexual exploitation. Prostitution falls under the umbrella, but the problem is much larger. Sex trafficking has become a global epidemic that threatens women's rights as well as their health. Victims must confront physical, psychological, and social challenges in addition to the inherent traumas.

Physical Challenges

The victims of sex trafficking are more prone to develop sexually transmitted diseases like syphilis, UTIs, or gonorrhea. Studies have also shown an increased risk of AIDS or HIV, although that weren't enough, it isn't uncommon for trafficked women to be abused, tortured, or kidnapped. Many are confined and deprived of food, which results in malnutrition.

Psychological Challenges

The abuse absorbed by women in sex trafficking can lead to severe psychological traumas. These vary but frequently include depression post traumatic stress disorder, or anxiety. Women who are stuck in the cycle suffer from instability, isolation and never ending fear. It is common for these women to also battle substance abuse addictions, either because they were hooked by their traffickers or because they turn to the drugs as a coping mechanism. It is essential for women who have been involved in sex trafficking to have access to mental health services.

Social Challenges

There are numerous indirect challenges faced by women because of sex trafficking. These women often experience poverty or homelessness. Few have friends or safety networks, so they suffer from social isolation. Many are denied an education and therefore are illiterate. These women lack essential resources and are therefore vulnerable to those who seek to enslave them.

After a woman falls into sex trafficking, it is nearly impossible to be saved without external assistance. Many of these women have been kidnapped from their homelands, and this results in confounding language barriers. They may also be trapped by fear, financial problems, or insufficient knowledge. If you or someone you know is a victim of sex trafficking, call the National Human Trafficking Resource Center:: 888.373.7888.

23. SINGLE MOTHERS

Giving birth and raising a child is always a challenge. People all over the world are buoyed down when faced with the responsibility of parenthood. But when you have your spouse at your side you feel a lot confident as you are assured of the presence of emotional support. Single parenting is a huge challenge in itself as you have lost your loved one and at the same time, you need to take up the responsibilities of rearing the child and life as a whole. Here are some common challenges faced by single mothers:

- The first challenge is to deal with the family all by yourself, where you need to fulfill the responsibility of both. You need to make all the decisions by yourself, you need to assure that all the requirements of the family are met. You need to deal with the overload of tasks that too efficiently, meet your career responsibilities and above all, deal with your emotional overload, not to overlook the emotional requirements of your baby.

- A single mom has to balance work and home all the more. Workplace is a whole new world of professional responsibilities. Then you need to take care of the children, provide them with all that they need, including your time and at the same time teach them to evolve as a disciplinarian by being a friend to them is an added challenge.

- Financial problems are some of the biggest problems faced by single moms. You cannot be a stay at home mom as you need to think of the expenses. Thereby you cannot spend all your time for rearing the child even if you believe that staying with the child throughout his growing years is important. The challenge magnifies if you are not very well off. It is a tough job to plan your entire expenses and yet have a savings through a single paycheck.

- Since you need to go to work you need to make adequate arrangement for childcare support. The person needs to be reliable as well as trustworthy. It is indeed a challenge to find such a person especially when you do not have a proper support system from your extended family.

The good side is that as the child grows up, your difficulties will fade away with the decrease of certain responsibilities which you can share with the child as his/her maturity level develops, he/she will also act as an emotional support that you so desperately crave for.

24. STRESS

The world of business today is very different from the world of business fifty years ago. Advances in technology plus the evolving work and family roles of women in this country have contributed to the business environment of the 21st century. The changing roles of women in America have led to their greater participation in the employment sector and changes in many aspects of American life. Women constitute 47 percent of the total labor.

Most women will remain in the paid labor force for 30 years. The typical American family today is the dual earner family. Women are now employed in previously male dominated fields, such as law, professional sports, the military, law enforcement, firefighting, and top level corporate positions. Working women today spend less time maintaining the household then they did 30 years ago. It had been anticipated that increased labor force participation for women and subsequent participation in multiple roles would result in increased stress. Research studies have actually determined that the opposite is true.

Stress can involve a recent change or a daily pressure. Stress happens to every one and can be motivating and productive or negative and destructive. Tension and anxiety, as well as depression, are frequently emotional consequences of stress.

The mind and body are linked throughout our lives. We must learn to respect both our emotional and physical needs, or we will lose our equilibrium and ability to adapt.

Symptoms of Stress

- Feeling tense
- Depression
- Poor memory
- Poor concentration
- Increased alcohol consumption
- Anger/hostility
- Difficulty making decisions
- Frequent mood swings
- Negative thinking
- Distractibility
- Excess smoking or eating
- Feeling overwhelmed or helpless

Stress increases the risk for

- Accidents
- Headaches
- Bowel disorders
- Poor digestion
- Skin disorders
- Eating disorders
- Emotional disorders
- Asthma attacks
- High blood pressure/strokes

- Colds/infections
- Backache
- Arthritis/immune disorders
- Heart attacks/recovery
- Cancer

Are women particularly susceptible to Stress?

Women are socialized to be the caretakers of others. More women than men have both a career outside the home and continue to try to juggle traditional responsibilities after hours. Over 70% of married women with children under the age of 18 are employed outside the home. Women are also less likely to be in powerful positions as men to change their environment. Women find it harder to say no to others' requests and often feel guilty if they can't please everyone. They often spend less time nurturing their own emotional and physical needs, as that might be perceived as selfish. In addition, relationship alterations or the loss of loved ones can produce empty nest or other separation syndromes.

As women progress through life's stages, hormonal balance associated with premenstrual, post partum and menopausal changes can affect chemical vulnerability to stress and depression.

How can I cope with Stress?

Leisure time must be considered a necessity, not just a reward for doing more. Personal time for rejuvenation will never be available unless it is planned. Prioritizing based on principle rather than demand is sometimes difficult to learn, but is critical for peace of mind.

You can't be all things to all people all of the time. Don't hesitate to ask for help. Avoid combining too many projects. Delegate if necessary. Learn to say 'no.'

What activities can help relieve Stress?

Here are some examples of activities that can help to refresh the body and mind.

- Taking baths
- Reading
- Doing breathing exercises
- Receiving back rubs/massages
- Listening to relaxation tapes
- Writing in a journal
- Meeting with a friend
- Napping
- Walking
- Dancing
- Engaging in spiritual reflection

25. WAR

Whether directly or indirectly affected, war causes suffering for women, often in unexpected ways. War challenges women as civilians, victims, combatants, and family members of combatants. They are often targeted because of their gender and inherent vulnerability. Some physically suffer from war crimes such as rape and torture, while others suffer emotionally, being separated from fathers, brothers, or spouses. In some regions, war withholds precious resources needed to survive. Females must develop strong coping skills to adjust to all of these challenges in a war torn world.

Female Soldiers

While females are often characterized as vulnerable, not all are passively affected by war. More and more women are volunteering to join the military ranks. Though more common then in the past, these women are challenged to succeed in a male dominated system while shrugging off the criticisms of those who openly protest a female presence in the military. Meanwhile, they risk their lives for the greater good.

Civilians

In the United States, most civilians are shielded from the ugliness of war, but this isn't the case elsewhere. Particularly in less developed nations, women and children find themselves victim to terrible violence as casualties of combat, rape, or wide scale bombing---bombs do not discriminate.

They also suffer indirectly through supply shortages. Women tend to take the bulk of the responsibility of taking care of their families or communities during war. Meanwhile, they are afflicted by fear and uncertainty. When their homelands are overrun, they are forced to choose between leaving everything they know behind or staying and risking their lives.

Mourning

The women who stay behind suffer do to the separation from loved ones. It is a difficult thing, not knowing where your loved one is, whether they are safe, or if they will come home unchanged. For too many, the separation becomes permanent and they find themselves challenged to pick up the pieces.

As a world superpower, the United States has a responsibility to safeguard the dignity and safety of females affected by war. The treaties drafted in terms of international humanitarian laws work towards this goal, but more than legislation is needed. Women continue to be challenged by the atrocities of war.

EPILOGUE

Women of destiny face challenges that can stifle their growth if they succumb to them. On the otherhand these challenges can strengthen them if they surmount them.

On life's bewildering journey a daily digest of the word of God and the leading of the Holy Spirit are essential to making the right decisions and walking in the right paths.

Women our steps are ordered and directed through the light of God's providence. In spite of the overwhelming circumstances---consider the following: *"And we know that all things work together for good to them that love God, to them who are the called according to his purpose." (Romans 8:28)*

Women, there are many roads in life, to ensure that we reach our destination, we must adhere to this proverbial injunction: *"Trust in the Lord with all thine heart; and lean not to thine own understanding. In all thine ways acknowledge Him and He shall direct thy paths." (Proverbs 3:5-6)*

In life there are tremendous challenges. *Nay, in all these things we are more than conqueror* s through Him that loved us." (Romans 8:37) We must confront these challenges and convert them into conquests---for God has called us to victory, success, and greatness. We can do it for we are anointed for greater works. (John 14:12)

BOOKS BY ELEANOR CRAWFORD:

- WOMEN IN MINISTRY: 25 WAYS TO IMPACT THE WORLD
- WOMEN OF DESTINY: 25 CHALLENGES WOMEN FACE
- WOMEN IN HISTORY: 25 WOMEN WHO CHANGED HISTORY
- WOMEN A MYSTERY: 25 FACTS ABOUT WOMEN

FORTHCOMING BOOKS BY ELEANOR CRAWFORD:

- WOMEN'S RESOURCES: 25 ASSETS
- WOMEN OF WISDOM: 25 INSIGHTS
- WOMEN'S MANUAL: 25 LIFE LESSONS
- WOMEN'S WORKBOOK: 25 ACTIVITIES
- WOMEN'S DEVOTIONAL BOOK
- WOMEN'S AFFIRMATION BOOK
- WOMEN'S SERMONS: 25 SERMONS
- WOMEN AND MEN: 25 CONTRASTS

BOOKS BY ALPHONSO CRAWFORD:

- LIFE'S WAY UNTIL: POEMS ON FAITH/HOPE/SALVATION
- TWO HEARTS: LOVE POEMS/LOVE LETTERS
- CROSSROADS: POEMS ON RACE/POLITICS/LIFE
- WISDOM: 25 FACTS ABOUT WISDOM
- TRIUMPHANT: 25 WAYS TO EXCEL IN LIFE

FORTHCOMING BOOKS BY ALPHONSO CRAWFORD:

- 100 WAYS FOR PEOPLE TO GET HEALED: VOLUMES 1-4
- 100 SYMBOLS OF HEALTH AND HEALING: VOLUMES 1-4
- ADVANCED HEALING MANUAL
- THE THREE GREATEST CHALLENGES OF LIFE
- DOMINATE: 25 DOMINION PRINCIPLES
- POWER: 25 FACTS ABOUT POWER
- WOMEN HAVE POWER: 25 POWERS WOMEN POSSESS
- WHY GOD MADE BLACK PEOPLE BLACK: 25 REASONS WHY
- LEADERSHIP IN AN AGE OF CRISIS: 25 OBSERVATIONS

MORE BOOKS

- LEADERSHIP: 25 PITFALLS/POWER TOOLS
- LEADERSHIP: 25 FACTS ABOUT LEADERS
- LEADERSHIP: TOUGH QUESTIONS/TOUGH ANSWERS
- GOD'S WILL: 25 WAYS TO KNOW GOD'S WILL FOR YOUR LIFE
- DREAMS: 25 FEATURES OF A DREAM
- ADVANCED INTERPERSONAL COMMUNICATION: 25 WAYS TO EXPRESS YOURSELF
- SPRITUOTHERAPY: 25 PRINCIPLES
- PERSONALITY PROFILES: A BIBLICAL PERSPECTIVE
- MEN: 25 FACTS ABOUT MEN
- HEALTH AND HEALING DEVOTIONAL BOOK
- HEALTH AND HEALING AFFIRMATION BOOK
- HEALTH AND HEALING WORKBOOK: 25 ACTIVITIES
- HEALTH AND HEALING QUIZ BOOK
- HEART: 25 FACTS ABOUT THE HEART
- BLOOD: 25 FACTS ABOUT BLOOD
- THE POWER OF BIG THINKING: 25 PRINCIPLES

BOOKS BY BYRON CRAWFORD:

- SUCCESS IN LIFE: 25 STEPS TO THE TOP
- LAWS OF SUCCESS: 25 LAWS
- SYNONYMS OF SUCCESS: 25 SYNONYMS
- SUCCESS UNLIMITED: 25 KEYS THAT UNLOCK DOORS

FORTHCOMING BOOKS BY BYRON CRAWFORD:

- SELL YOUR WAY TO SUCCESS: 25 WAYS TO SUCCEED IN LIFE
- SECRETS OF SUCCESS: 25 SECRETS
- SUCCESS MANUAL: 25 LIFE LESSONS
- SUCCESS WORKBOOK: 25 ACTIVITIES
- SUCCESSFUL STRATEGIC PLANNING: 25 TACTICS
- SUCCESS SERMONS: 25 SERMONS
- SUCCESS QUIZ BOOK
- SUCCESS DEVOTIONAL BOOK
- SUCCESS AFFIRMATION BOOK

SIGN UP AND BE NOTIFIED FOR SEMINARS/WORKSHOPS/CONFERENCES

NAME _____

ADDRESS _____

CITY _____

STATE _____

ZIP CODE _____

PHONE NO . _____

EMAIL _____

SEND TO:

NEW LIFE EDUCATIONAL SERVICES
P.O. BOX 96
OAK LAWN, ILLINOIS 60454

SEMINARS / WORKSHOPS / CONFERENCES

- ANNUAL WOMEN'S LUNCHEON
- ANNUAL MEN'S LUNCHEON
- HEALTH AND HEALING
- DREAMS AND VISIONS
- PERSONAL POWER
- GIFTS AND TALENTS
- PROBLEM SOLVING
- RELATIONSHIPS
- INTERPRETING CURRENT TRENDS
- ADVANCED COMMUNICATION
- ADVANCED STRATEGIC PLANNING
- MANAGING SELF
- MANAGING CONFLICT
- MANAGING STRESS
- LAWS OF POWER
- NEGOTIATION SKILLS
- BIG THINKING POWER
- STRATEGIES FOR SUCCESS
- HOW TO SELL YOURSELF
- GLOBAL STEWARDSHIP
- HOW TO COUNSEL
- SELF MOTIVATION

- PEOPLE MOTIVATION
- APOSTOLIC/PROPHETIC CONFERENCE
- TEAM BUILDING
- VISION
- TIME MANAGEMENT
- SETTING GOALS
- CHANGE AGENTS
- WEALTH IN YOU
- FEEDBACK
- NEEDS OF MEN AND WOMEN
- SELF DECEPTION: HOW WE LIE TO OURSELVES EVERYDAY
- HOW TO START A CHRISTIAN SCHOOL
- HOW TO HOME SCHOOL
- LIFE SKILLS

ABOUT THE AUTHOR

Eleanor has remarkable leadership skills. She is an outstanding speaker that projects all the sophistication, graces, and charms of an ambassador of Christ. Women are encouraged to passionately pursue their dreams while they engage themselves in kingdom ministry. Eleanor pastors with her husband at Cathedral Of Prayer. Her goals are directed towards one end, fulfilling the spiritual mandate that God has given her.

Eleanor has a Bachelor of Arts Degree from Chicago State University, a Master Of Divinity Degree and a Doctor Of Ministry Degree from Cathedral Theological Seminary.